BENJAMIN FRANKLIN

by Ellis M. Reed

Cody Koala

An Imprint of Pop!
popbooksonline.com

abdopublishing.com
Published by Pop!, a division of ABDO, PO Box 398166, Minneapolis, Minnesota 55439.

Printed in the United States of America, North Mankato, Minnesota

032018
092018

THIS BOOK CONTAINS RECYCLED MATERIALS

Cover Photo: iStockphoto
Interior Photos: iStockphoto, 1, 9, 13, 19 (right), 21 (bottom right); Joseph-Siffrède Duplessis/Library of Congress, 5 (top); North Wind Picture Archives, 5 (left), 6, 14, 21 (bottom left); Shutterstock Images, 5 (right), 10, 16–17, 19 (left), 19 (top), 21 (top)

Editor: Charly Haley
Series Designer: Laura Mitchell

Library of Congress Control Number: 2017963379

Publisher's Cataloging-in-Publication Data
Names: Reed, Ellis M., author.
Title: Benjamin Franklin / by Ellis M. Reed.
Description: Minneapolis, Minnesota : Pop!, 2019. | Series: Founding fathers | Includes online resources and index.
Identifiers: ISBN 9781532160189 (lib.bdg.) | ISBN 9781532161308 (ebook) |
Subjects: LCSH: Franklin, Benjamin, 1706-1790--Juvenile literature. | Founding Fathers of the United States--Juvenile literature. | Statesmen--United States--Biography--Juvenile literature. | United States--Politics and government--1783-1789--Juvenile literature.
Classification: DDC 973.4 [B]--dc23

Hello! My name is

Cody Koala

Pop open this book and you'll find QR codes like this one, loaded with information, so you can learn even more!

Scan this code* and others like it while you read, or visit the website below to make this book pop.

popbooksonline.com/benjamin-franklin

*Scanning QR codes requires a web-enabled smart device with a QR code reader app and a camera.

Table of Contents

Chapter 1

Growing Up

Benjamin Franklin grew up in Boston. The city was part of the Massachusetts Bay **colony** in America. The colony was controlled by Great Britain.

Watch a video here!

Benjamin went to school until he was 10 years old. He then worked as a **printer**. He taught himself to write well. Benjamin started his own newspaper in 1729.

Benjamin had 16 siblings!

Chapter 2

War

Franklin wrote many papers during the **American Revolutionary War**. The American colonies fought to be separate from Great Britain.

Learn more here!

IN CONGRESS, JULY 4,
Declaration of the thirteen united States of

Franklin was one of five people who helped write the **Declaration of Independence**. This said America was its own country.

Chapter 3

Colonies to Country

Franklin helped write a treaty in 1783 that ended the Revolutionary War. The United States became a country, separate from Great Britain.

Learn more here!

Franklin

Americans argued about how the new country should work. Franklin helped write the **Constitution**. It had rules for the new country.

Franklin was the oldest person who helped create the Constitution. He was 81 years old.

Franklin was an inventor. He flew a kite in a thunderstorm. The kite had a key attached to it.

This experiment helped Franklin invent the lightning rod.

Chapter 4

America Today

Franklin died in 1790. Today, many schools and buildings are named after him.

Complete an activity here!

Franklin was a **Founding Father**. He helped shape the United States. We still use the Constitution today.

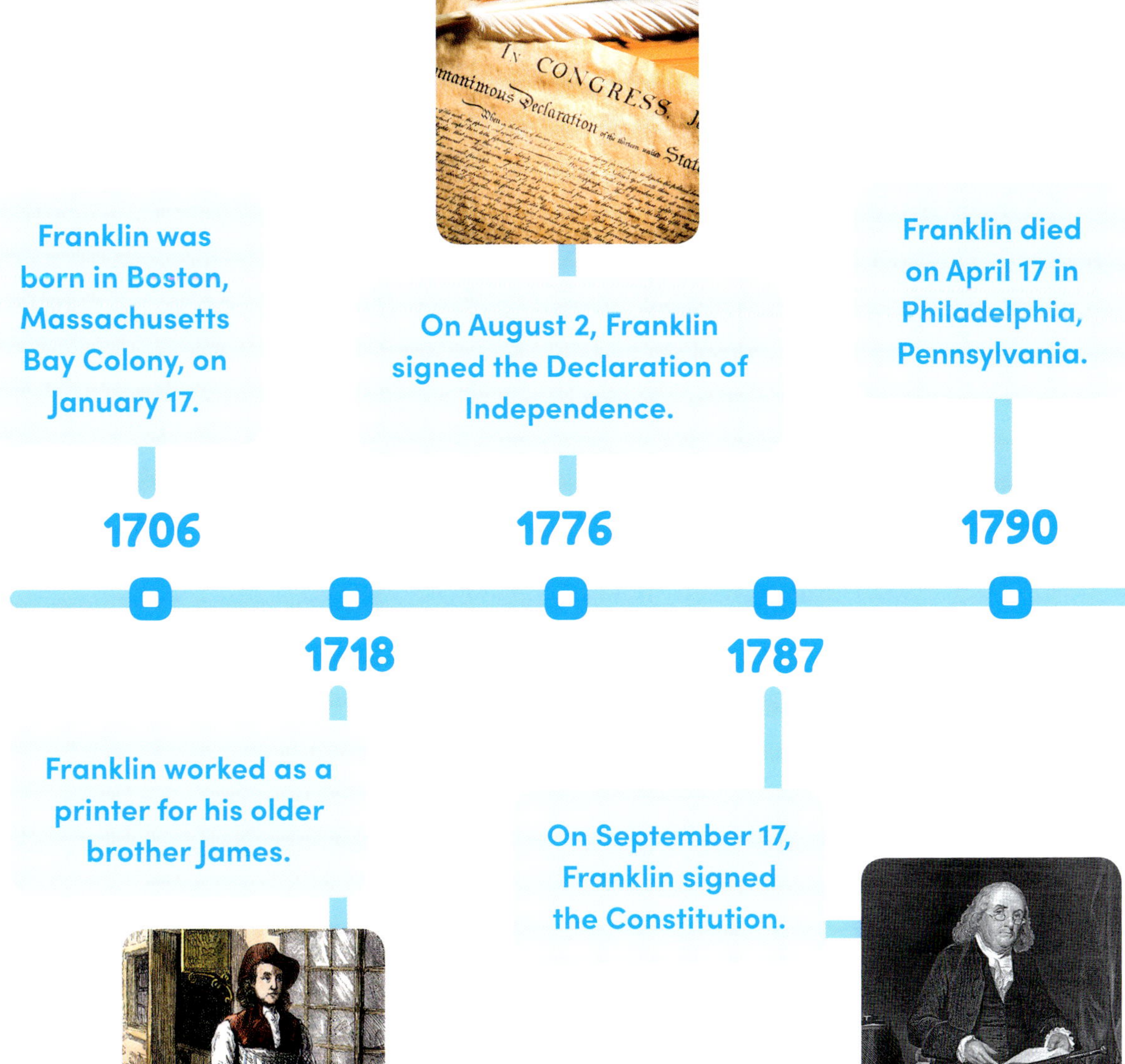
IN CONGRESS
unanimous Declaration
Franklin was born in Boston, Massachusetts Bay Colony, on January 17.
1706
Franklin worked as a printer for his older brother James.
1718
On August 2, Franklin signed the Declaration of Independence.
1776
On September 17, Franklin signed the Constitution.
1787
Franklin died on April 17 in Philadelphia, Pennsylvania.
1790

Making Connections

Text-to-Self

Franklin wrote many things. What do you like to write?

Text-to-Text

Have you read another book about the Constitution? Were there other people who helped write the Constitution?

Text-to-World

Franklin was a Founding Father. How did his actions in the past help make the world you live in today?

Glossary

American Revolutionary War – the war fought between the colonies and Great Britain.

colony – a land ruled by another country.

Constitution – a set of rules about what the US government can do.

Declaration of Independence – a document that said America is its own country.

Founding Father – one of the people who helped create the US government.

printer – a person who worked to print reading material such as newspapers and books.

Index

Online Resources

popbooksonline.com

Thanks for reading this Cody Koala book!

Scan this code* and others like it in this book, or visit the website below to make this book pop!

popbooksonline.com/benjamin-franklin

*Scanning QR codes requires a web-enabled smart device with a QR code reader app and a camera.